Countries Around the World

United States of America

Michael Hurley

Heinemann Library
Chicago, Illinois

www.capstonepub.com
Visit our website to find out more information about Heinemann-Raintree books.

To order:
☎ Phone 888-454-2279
🖥 Visit www.capstonepub.com to browse our catalog and order online.

Edited by Catherine Veitch and Charlotte Guillain
Designed by Steve Mead
Original illustrations © Capstone Global Library Ltd 2012
Illustrated by Oxford Designers & Illustrators
Picture research by Hannah Taylor
Originated by Capstone Global Library, Ltd.
Printed in China by CTPS

15 14 13 12 11
10 9 8 7 6 5 4 3 2 1

Library of Congress Cataloging-in-Publication Data
Hurley, Michael.
  United States of America / Michael Hurley.
    p. cm.—(Countries around the world)
  Includes bibliographical references and index.
  ISBN 978-1-4329-6115-2 (hb)—ISBN 978-1-4329-6141-1 (pb) 1.
United States—Juvenile literature. 2. United States—History—Juvenile literature. I. Title.
  E156.H93 2012
  973—dc23   2011015809

Acknowledgments
We would like to thank the following for permission to reproduce photographs: Corbis pp. 12 (Wally McNamee), 13 (Bob Adelman), 23 (Tyrone Turner/National Geographic Society), 26 (Robin Nelson/ZUMA Press), 29 (Tom Fox/Dallas Morning News), 31 (Hulton-Deutsch Collection), 32 (Bettmann), 35 (Irwin Thompson/Dallas Morning News); Getty Images pp. 7 (Bridgeman Art Library), 22 (AFP/Saul Loeb), 34 (Joe Robbins); Istockphoto pp. 15 (© Richard Gunion), 16 (© Tomasz Szymanski), 27 (© jabejon); The Kobal Collection p. 33 (UNIVERSAL/DREAM-WORKS); Library of Congress pp. 9, 10, 11; Shutterstock pp. 5 (© Songquan Deng), 6 (© stocksnapp), 8 (© Susan Law Cain), 19 (© egd), 20 (© Ferenc Cegledi), 21 (© Andrew S.), 25 (© Christopher Halloran), 39 (© S.Borisov).

Cover photograph of the Statue of Liberty reproduced with permission of Corbis (Cameron Davidson).

Every effort has been made to contact copyright holders of material reproduced in this book. Any omissions will be rectified in subsequent printings if notice is given to the publisher.

The publishers would like to thank Dr. Elizabeth Clapp and Marta Segal Block for their assistance in the preparation of this book. The author would also like to thank Catherine Clarke for her assistance with this book.

Disclaimer
All the Internet addresses (URLs) given in this book were valid at the time of going to press. However, due to the dynamic nature of the Internet, some addresses may have changed, or sites may have changed or ceased to exist since publication. While the author and publisher regret any inconvenience this may cause readers, no responsibility for any such changes can be accepted by either the author or the publisher.

Contents

Introducing the United States of America...............................4

History: Exploration, Colonization, and Conflict...................6

Regions and Resources: Mountains,

 Manufacturing, and Movies 14

Wildlife: Diversity and Disasters 20

Infrastructure: Leaders, Health, and Schools 24

Culture: Food, Sports, and Entertainment......................28

The United States Today..34

Fact File 36

Timeline 40

Glossary 42

Find Out More 44

Topic Tools 46

Index 48

Some words in the book are in bold, **like this**. You can find out what they mean by looking in the glossary.

Introducing the United States of America

What comes to mind when you think of the United States of America? Do you see the U.S. flag, with its stars and stripes? Do you think of big cities with towering skyscrapers, or dramatic landscapes like the Grand Canyon? Or maybe movie stars or sports stars?

North America

The United States is an enormous and varied country. Its stunning scenery includes dramatic coastlines, mountain ranges, forests, deserts, rivers, and lakes. The United States is part of the **continent** of North America, which also includes Canada and Mexico. After Canada, the United States is the second-largest country on the continent. It has an area of more than 3,794,100 square miles (9,826,675 square kilometers). The population of the United States is approximately 307 million, making it the third most populated country in the world. The culture of the country shows great **diversity**, with people from all around the world settling there.

Superpower

The United States is often referred to as a superpower. This refers to the strength of its government and its influence over the rest of the world. In terms of size, population, and **economy**, the United States has been a very powerful country for over a century. The United States is often at the forefront of international efforts, whether in response to a natural disaster such as an earthquake or to the outbreak of war between two countries. This influence on a global scale creates both positive and negative feelings toward the country.

Many U.S. cities have amazing skylines full of tall buildings.

History: Exploration, Colonization, and Conflict

Humans have lived in the land that is now the United States for more than 12,000 years. Over time these people settled all over what is now North America. These people, who later became known as American Indians, or Native Americans, lived here for thousands of years before other settlers arrived on the **continent**.

Daily life

American Indians made tools and hunted for food. Coastal people lived on a diet of mainly fish, while inland **tribes** hunted animals such as bison (buffalo) for meat. Different tribes developed their own religions and cultures.

Discovering a "new world"

From the 1400s, explorers, including Christopher Columbus, set off from Europe. They explored new lands in the Caribbean and the coasts of Central and South America. In 1497 John Cabot, an Italian navigator sailing on a British ship, became the first European to visit the northeast coast of North America since the Vikings in 1000 CE.

Colonization

The first permanent British settlement in North America was Jamestown, which was founded in 1607 in present-day Virginia. Between 1620 and 1630 more **colonists** arrived on the northeastern coast. The British people who **migrated** here were known as Puritans. They wanted to come to this new land because they thought that they would be free to practice their religion in their own way.

The early colonists faced many hardships and dangers. Food was often scarce and disease was common. They also came into conflict with American Indian people. The American Indians helped and supported the colonists—until their lands and way of life became threatened. Eventually, the colonists managed to establish farms and plantations.

This is an artist's impression of an early British settlement on the east coast of North America.

In CONGRESS, JULY 4, 1776.

The unanimous Declaration of the thirteen united States of America,

The Declaration of Independence was adopted on July 4, 1776.

The American Revolution

The new settlers built up thriving settlements, and they began to resent the restrictions imposed on their freedom by the British. On April 19, 1775, the Revolutionary War began between the Americans and the British. In 1783 the Americans finally defeated the British.

Territorial expansion

In 1803 the United States bought land from the French in the Louisiana Purchase. For about $15 million, the United States acquired land that went from New Orleans in the south to Montana in the north. This encouraged more American citizens to move westward.

War broke out between the United States and Mexico in 1846 over land ownership and boundaries. U.S. forces invaded Mexico and eventually gained lands that included present-day New Mexico and California. The United States now controlled land from the east coast to the west coast.

Civil War (1861–1865)

From the 1500s, many Africans were taken from their homes and forced to work in the growing European settlements in North America. By the 1800s, slavery was a part of life in the United States, and it became a major factor in the most devastating war in U.S. history.

The Civil War ripped the nation in half. The southern Confederate states fought to protect slavery and break away from the northern states. The northern Union states wanted to preserve the union and end slavery. This terrible war divided the country, and families and friends fought on opposite sides. More than 620,000 soldiers were killed.

HARRIET TUBMAN

(ABOUT 1820–1913)

Harriet Tubman was an escaped slave. She helped many other slaves to escape to freedom in the North and Canada. During the Civil War, she served as a nurse and spy for the Union Army.

Boom time

There were huge developments in industry after the Civil War. An increase in machine-operated manufacturing was driven by new inventions and railroad networks. The industrial growth caused a boom in the **economy** that continued into the 1900s.

World War I

The United States stayed out of World War I (1914–18) at first, but President Woodrow Wilson and the American people were moved to join the war against Germany in 1917. Around two million soldiers were sent across the Atlantic to help the **Allies** to victory in 1918.

The 1920s and the Great Depression

The 1920s are often known as the "Roaring Twenties" because of the booming economy and fast-paced life Americans experienced at that time. But by the end of the 1920s, the spectacular economic growth had become unstable, and in 1929 the **stock market** crashed.

During the Great Depression in the 1930s, people were forced to line up for hours to get food.

During the Great Depression, which followed this crash, banks failed, millions of workers lost their jobs, and thousands of farmers were forced to abandon their farms. In 1933 around 13 million Americans were out of work.

World War II

The United States initially stayed out of World War II (1939–45). However, in 1941 a devastating Japanese attack on a U.S. naval base at Pearl Harbor brought the country into the war. At the time of the attack, Japan's ally, Germany, had taken over much of Europe. So the United States joined the Allies, which included the United Kingdom and the **Soviet Union**, to defeat their enemies. The war ended in 1945, when the United States dropped **atomic** bombs on two Japanese cities, Hiroshima and Nagasaki.

The surprise attack on Pearl Harbor by the Japanese cost over 2,000 U.S. lives. It led directly to the United States' involvement in World War II.

The Cold War and Vietnam

Following World War II, a Cold War developed between the **capitalist** and **communist** nations of the world. This tension was mainly between the United States and the Soviet Union. The Cold War led to conflict in other countries, where the United States was eager to prevent the rise of communism. One of the major conflicts was the Vietnam War (1954–75), in Southeast Asia. Thousands of people were killed in this war, and many Americans protested against it.

During the Vietnam War, protesters marched in Washington, D.C., to make their point. They wanted the war to end and U.S. soldiers to return home.

JOHN F. KENNEDY (1917–1963)

John F. Kennedy was the youngest man ever to be elected president of the United States, and he was also the youngest to die in office. He was assassinated in 1963, and the nation mourned the passing of the popular young leader.

Civil rights

After the end of the Civil War and the **abolition** of slavery, **segregation** laws remained in the United States, including "Jim Crow laws" in the South. These laws prevented white and black people from using the same public places, such as public bathrooms and drinking fountains.

In 1955, in Alabama, an African American woman named Rosa Parks refused to give up her seat on a public bus for a white person. She was arrested and fined, creating headlines across the country. This started a **civil rights** movement to end segregation. For many years the fight for civil rights was led by Dr. Martin Luther King, Jr. He encouraged people to protest peacefully rather than turn to violence. Tragically, he was **assassinated** in 1968. Gradually, attitudes changed, and in 2008 the people of the United States elected their first non-white president, Barack Obama.

The 1960s were a time of turmoil in the United States. There were many protest marches by African Americans trying to get equal rights.

Regions and Resources: Mountains, Manufacturing, and Movies

The United States is the third-largest country in the world by area. It has a land border with Canada to the north, and with Mexico to the south. Two of the states, Alaska and Hawaii, are not physically linked to the rest of the United States. Alaska is in the far northwest of North America, bordering Canada. Hawaii is an island group in the Pacific Ocean.

Climate

Due to the size of the country, the climate in the United States varies greatly from region to region. From the hot and dry deserts of Arizona, to the freezing subarctic landscape of Alaska, the United States has almost every type of climate there is on Earth! The United States is used to extreme weather, including hurricanes and tornadoes.

This map shows the physical features, such as mountains and rivers, of the United States.

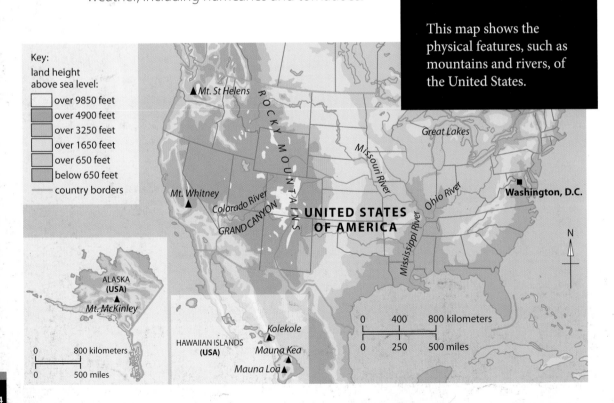

Key:
land height above sea level:
- over 9850 feet
- over 4900 feet
- over 3250 feet
- over 1650 feet
- over 650 feet
- below 650 feet
- country borders

Mt. St Helens
ROCKY MOUNTAINS
Great Lakes
Missouri River
Mt. Whitney
Colorado River
GRAND CANYON
Ohio River
UNITED STATES OF AMERICA
Mississippi River
Washington, D.C.
N

ALASKA (USA)
Mt. McKinley
0   800 kilometers
0   500 miles

HAWAIIAN ISLANDS (USA)
Kolekole
Mauna Kea
Mauna Loa

0   400   800 kilometers
0   250   500 miles

Key landforms

The landscape of the United States includes mountains and tropical areas, as well as huge plains and large deserts. It has one of the longest coastlines in the world.

The Grand Canyon, in Arizona, is one of the most spectacular landforms in the world. It was formed over millions of years by the Colorado River. The canyon extends 277 miles (446 kilometers) and is approximately 1 mile (1.6 kilometers) deep. At 20,322 feet (6,194 meters), the country's highest mountain is Mount McKinley, in Alaska.

Mount McKinley was named after President William McKinley. The Athabaskan Indians of Alaska, however, called the mountain Denali, which means "The Great One" or "The High One."

States

Fifty states make up the United States. Alaska is the largest state, with an area of 591,006 square miles (1,530,699 square kilometers). This is more than twice the size of the next largest state, Texas. The smallest state is Rhode Island, with an area of 1,212 square miles (3,139 square kilometers). Each state has its own identity, including its own capital city and flag.

Major cities

The capital city of the United States is Washington, D.C. It is home to many important government buildings, including the White House, the residence of the president. The two largest cities in the United States are New York City, on the east coast, and Los Angeles, California, on the west coast. Both cities have large, **multicultural** populations.

The United States' third-largest city is Chicago. Chicago is in the state of Illinois, on the edge of Lake Michigan. It is a beautiful city with lakefront beaches, large parks, and the world-famous Art Institute of Chicago.

Chicago is known as the "Windy City." This is because of the strong winds that blow off Lake Michigan.

How to say...

As people from the United States come from all over the world, many languages are spoken. In addition to English, the most commonly spoken languages are Spanish, Chinese, **Tagalog**, Vietnamese, and French. Here are some basic greetings in Spanish:

hello	*hola*	(oh-lah)
goodbye	*adiós*	(ah-dee-os)
my name is…	*mi llamo…*	(may yamo)
thank you	*gracias*	(grah-see-ahs)
good night	*buenos noches*	(bway-nos no-chays)

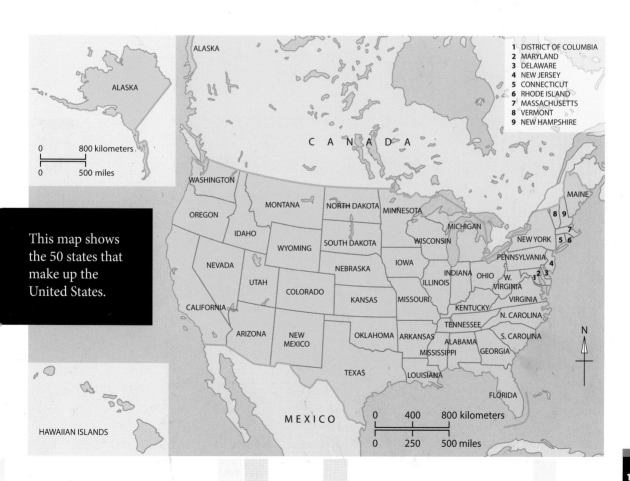

This map shows the 50 states that make up the United States.

1 DISTRICT OF COLUMBIA
2 MARYLAND
3 DELAWARE
4 NEW JERSEY
5 CONNECTICUT
6 RHODE ISLAND
7 MASSACHUSETTS
8 VERMONT
9 NEW HAMPSHIRE

Economy

The U.S. **economy** is one of the strongest in the world. There are many different industries in different parts of the country.

Manufacturing

Traditionally, large parts of the Midwest have been industrial areas, producing steel, cars, and machinery. The city of Detroit, Michigan, for example, produces more cars each year than any other part of the country and is known as "Motor City." The city's location on the Detroit River played a large part in its rapid growth, as it was cheap and easy to transport **raw materials** to Detroit.

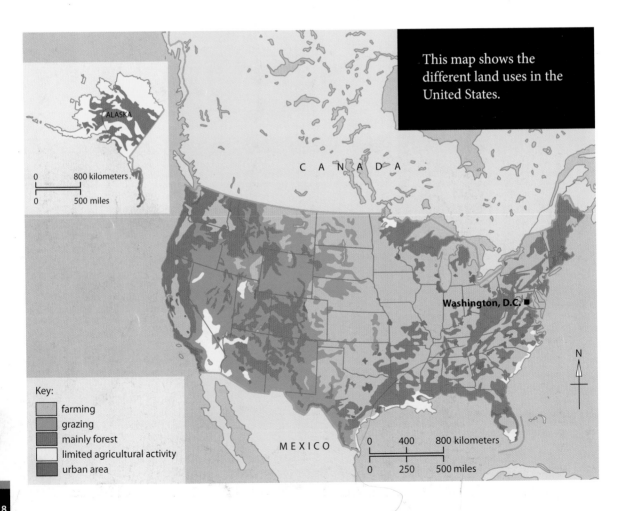

This map shows the different land uses in the United States.

ALASKA

0   800 kilometers

0   500 miles

CANADA

Washington, D.C. ■

N

Key:
- farming
- grazing
- mainly forest
- limited agricultural activity
- urban area

MEXICO

0   400   800 kilometers

0   250   500 miles

Agriculture

Alongside manufacturing, agriculture still remains a huge industry for the United States. Kansas is one of the largest producers of wheat in the country and is often called the "Breadbasket of America." The fertile soil and rich mineral deposits make Kansas an ideal farming area, and farmland covers 90 percent of the state, including around 63,000 farms.

Sunshine industry

The west coast of the United States is famous for its movie industry. Hollywood, California, became a center of the movie industry because it has a mild, dry climate, plus it offers a huge variety of natural scenery that can be used for filming. The movie industry contributes millions of dollars to the U.S. economy each year. The San Francisco Bay Area, in northern California, is home to "Silicon Valley." This is the leading computer-manufacturing region of the country, and it includes the headquarters of hundreds of computer and electronics companies, such as Apple and Hewlett-Packard.

Hollywood, California, is one of the most famous and fascinating places on Earth.

Wildlife: Diversity and Disasters

Due to the country's size and the different types of land and climate across the United States, there is a rich variety of plant and animal life.

In Alaska, for example, there is a great **diversity** of arctic wildlife. The region is home to 180 bird **species**, around 45 types of land and marine mammals (including grizzly and polar bears), and more than 35 types of fish. Many of these animals are not found anywhere else in the United States. Unfortunately, the natural **habitats** in this area are under threat from climate change and the activities of oil companies.

In the far southern part of the country, in Florida, the Everglades are home to very different wildlife. Plant life ranges from saw grass to mangrove swamps. Animals in the Everglades include alligators, heron, pelicans, and snakes. There is also the rare Florida panther to look out for!

Alligators live in swamps in Florida and Louisiana. These alligators are often hunted for their meat and their skin.

National parks

There are national parks all over the United States. These parks are areas specifically set up to protect the natural environment. There are 393 parks in 49 states, covering a total area of 131,250 square miles (339,936 square kilometers). In 2009 there were almost three million visitors to the national parks.

Yellowstone National Park stretches across three states: Wyoming, Montana, and Idaho. Visitors can see animals such as wolves, bison, elk, and grizzly bears in their natural environment. Another big draw for visitors are the amazing **geysers** that spray hot water from underground up into the air.

People travel from all over the world to visit Yellowstone National Park. They want to catch a glimpse of the largest geyser, "Old Faithful," in action.

Environmental disasters

Two of the most damaging environmental disasters in U.S. history have involved oil spills. In 1989 the *Exxon Valdez* oil tanker struck a reef in Prince William Sound, Alaska, spilling nearly 11 million gallons (42 million liters) of oil into the sea. This destroyed wildlife and polluted beaches and fishing waters. Scientists are still working to restore the ecological balance in this area.

On April 20, 2010, the Deepwater Horizon oil rig in the Gulf of Mexico exploded, killing 11 workers. It then sank, causing 5,000 barrels of oil per day to leak into the ocean. Wildlife, including brown pelicans, ducks, turtles, and whales, were affected as they got caught up in the slick, and coastal industries were severely affected.

A volunteer at the Fort Jackson Oiled Wildlife Rehabilitation Center in Buras, Louisiana, cleans an oil-covered pelican. It was found off the Louisiana coast.

Pollution and waste

Fossil fuels are fuels such as coal and oil that are burned for fuel. When they are burned, they give off harmful substances like carbon dioxide, which are called greenhouse gases. Scientists believe that greenhouse gases lead to global warming, a worldwide rise in temperatures. The United States releases more carbon dioxide than any other country in the world. As a result, there is increasing pressure for the country to find ways to reduce this problem.

Like many other **developed countries**, the United States creates a huge amount of waste. A U.S. citizen creates two to three times the amount of waste as a person living in a **developing country**. In 2005 the United States created 246 million tons of garbage! However, recycling has increased, and from 1990 to 2005 the amount of waste going to landfills decreased by 9 million tons. Environmentalists want to see more people recycling, composting, and reusing their garbage.

It is very important that families recycle as much waste as possible.

Infrastructure: Leaders, Health, and Schools

The system of government in the United States divides power between the national government and individual state governments. This is called **federalism**. Each state has many powers that would be the responsibility of the national government in many countries. For example, states are responsible for creating many laws, including setting their own state taxes.

BARACK OBAMA (BORN 1961)

Barack Obama is the first non-white president of the United States. He was born to a Kenyan father and white U.S. mother in Hawaii. Obama worked as a state senator in Illinois and as a U.S. senator from Illinois, before becoming the Democratic Party's nominee for the 2008 presidential election.

National government

The two main political parties in the United States are the Republican Party and the Democratic Party. Every four years, each party chooses a representative, and these two candidates compete for the presidency. Third-party candidates often also enter the race. Once elected, a president can be in power for no more than two terms, for a maximum of eight years.

The U.S. **Congress** is made up of the House of Representatives and the **Senate**. The Senate has 100 members, two from each state, and the House of Representatives has 435. The number of members from each state in the House of Representatives is based on the size of each state's population.

Health care

In the United States, people must pay for their own health care. This is done by buying insurance, which helps pay for medication and treatment. Many people have insurance through their jobs, but others do not have insurance and cannot afford medical care. The U.S. government is currently trying to change this health care system.

U.S. President Barack Obama is shown here addressing the nation.

School life

Each state has control over its own education system and decides what students will study at school. At the age of five, many children start kindergarten. This prepares children for school. From the age of six, children begin more formal education, studying subjects such as math, science, and social studies. They then go on to either a middle school or a junior high school.

Students then study the required subjects of English, math, science, and health in high school. Additionally, they can choose some classes from either a college preparatory or a **vocational** curriculum.

Many school children start their day in class by reciting the "Pledge of Allegiance," which is a solemn promise to be loyal to their country, while saluting the U.S. flag.

These students are reciting the Pledge of Allegiance at the start of a school day.

Daily life

The school day usually starts at about 8:00 a.m. and ends at about 3:00 p.m. Many schools operate a school bus service to take students to and from school. The yellow school bus is a familiar sight and is something that is recognized around the world as a symbol of U.S. school life.

College

High school is the end of required education in the United States, but some students continue their education in college. The United States has many famous colleges, including Harvard and Yale. Many students who cannot afford to go to college or who are not academically ready start at a junior college and later transfer to a larger university.

Culture: Food, Sports, and Entertainment

For many generations, people have moved to the United States in search of opportunity. This has created a **multicultural** population with a rich mixture of customs and cultures.

Food

Many large American cities have areas called "Chinatown" or "Little Italy," where restaurants serve food from those countries. There is a culture of eating out, with hundreds of restaurants in every city. Some are fast food restaurants. People also often cook at home. People have family meals at home to celebrate special occasions, such as Thanksgiving, and they have cookouts during the summer.

Chocolate brownies

Ask an adult to help you make these delicious treats.

Ingredients
- 1/4 cup softened margarine
- 1/4 cup sugar
- 1/2 cup unsweetened cocoa powder
- 1 egg
- 3/4 cup all-purpose flour
- 1/4 cup chopped walnuts

What to do
1. Preheat the oven to 350°F (180°C).
2. Lightly grease a 3.5-by-7.5-inch (8-by-20-centimeter) cookie sheet.
3. Cream the margarine and sugar together in a large bowl.
4. Mix in the cocoa powder, then add the egg and beat the mixture for about 1 to 2 minutes, until smooth and combined.
5. Sift the flour and add to the mixture, then stir in the nuts.
6. Evenly spread the mixture into the pan and bake for 18 to 20 minutes.
7. Cool and then cut into squares.

Sports

Many major U.S. cities have professional sports teams that play baseball, football, basketball, and ice hockey. Fans enthusiastically follow these teams. Each sport has a season, and these seasons overlap, so there are always sports being played. Each sport has an end-of-season game, or series of games, to decide who is the overall winner for the year. In baseball this is called the World Series, while in football it is the Super Bowl.

MICHAEL JORDAN (BORN 1963)

Michael Jordan is one of the best-known athletes in the United States. He was the most influential and talented player for the Chicago Bulls basketball team. His team won six National Basketball Association (NBA) titles.

The United States has many great athletes who compete on a world stage, in competitions such as the Olympics.

Music

The United States has a very rich musical history. The earliest popular music was traditional folk music, which originated in Europe and other parts of the world. Musical styles that first appeared in the United States include gospel, jazz, country, blues, and rock 'n' roll.

In the 1950s and 1960s, rock 'n' roll was popular. Elvis Presley became famous around the world. Modern music has many different cultural influences. Rap music and R&B include songs that tell stories about **urban** life. Dance, pop, and rock music are still very popular with people of all ages and backgrounds.

Theater

The most famous theater district in the United States is Broadway, in New York City. Many plays and long-running musicals are performed here, attracting New Yorkers and out-of-town visitors alike. This theater district has its own annual awards ceremony, the Tony Awards, which honors achievement in areas such as acting, directing, designing, musical arrangements, and choreography (creating dance routines).

Visual art

Andy Warhol and Jackson Pollock are two famous U.S. artists. Both were controversial figures during their careers, but they are now considered two of the greatest artists of the last century. Warhol's prints present everyday objects, such as cans of soup, in a new and visually stimulating way. Pollock's style used aggressive strokes and paint dripped directly onto a canvas.

This is Ella Fitzgerald recording [on]e of her songs. She made her [fir]st recording, called "Love and [Ki]sses," in 1935.

ELLA FITZGERALD (1917–1996)

Ella Fitzgerald, known as "the first lady of song," was one of the greatest jazz singers of all time. She was popular with people of different races, ages, and backgrounds. In a career that lasted more than 50 years, she sold over 40 million albums and won many awards.

Movies

Movies are a huge part of life for many Americans. Many movies are made in Hollywood. The first movies were black-and-white silent films that were usually comedies. As technology moved on, sound and color were introduced. From musicals to westerns, Hollywood produced some of the best-known and best-loved movies of all time.

WALT DISNEY (1901–1966)

Cartoons and animated movies have always been popular, and none more so than those created by Walt Disney. He created characters such as Mickey Mouse and Donald Duck. His full-length movies, including *Fantasia*, *The Jungle Book*, and *Mary Poppins*, helped him to win an amazing 32 Academy Awards!

One of the most successful movies of all time was the 1939 epic *Gone with the Wind*, which was set against the backdrop of the Civil War. This movie was based on a novel by author Margaret Mitchell.

Literature

One of the best-known U.S. authors of the 1800s was Mark Twain, who wrote *The Adventures of Huckleberry Finn*. Millions of children and adults have enjoyed this adventure set along the Mississippi River.

Louisa May Alcott's novel *Little Women* tells the story of a group of sisters growing up in New England in the mid-1800s. It has been made into several movies.

From *The Grinch* to *The Cat in the Hat*, children's author Dr. Seuss created some of the best-loved characters in literature. His clever rhyming text and funny illustrations have charmed many children over the years, and in 1984 the Pulitzer Prize Board awarded him a special honor "for his contribution over nearly half a century to the education and enjoyment of America's children and their parents."

Dr. Seuss' creation *The Cat in the Hat* was turned into a movie in 2003.

The United States Today

The United States is an ever-changing country, and its major cities continue to grow in size and population. The influx of people from other countries means that there is great **diversity** in its population.

The United States is a very strong country from a political point of view. It is a member of the **G8** and the **United Nations**. It works closely with other **developed countries** to find solutions to worldwide problems such as hunger and terrorism. The United States also has an important trade agreement with Canada and Mexico, called the North American Free Trade Agreement (NAFTA). This ensures fairness for the three countries in terms of the **import** and **export** of their goods.

Americans express national pride in many ways. The national anthem, the "Star Spangled Banner," is sung before all major sporting events.

Resilience

The people of the United States often show strength in the face of challenges. When disaster strikes, they come together to help each other.

The events of September 11, 2001, when four airplanes were hijacked by **terrorists**, were the first time since the Japanese attack on Pearl Harbor that the United States had been attacked on home soil. The destruction caused by planes flying into the World Trade Center in New York and the **Pentagon** sent shockwaves through the country, and the world. The ability of the U.S. people, particularly New Yorkers, to withstand such a tragic event and continue with their lives has shown their great determination and courage.

After Hurricane Katrina devastated the city of New Orleans in 2005, people from all over the world helped to raise money to assist those affected.

Many thousands of people in New Orleans were made homeless because of the devastating impact of the flooding after Hurricane Katrina.

Fact File

Official name:	United States of America
Official language:	English (Hawaiian is the official language of the state of Hawaii)
Capital city:	Washington, D.C.
Bordering countries:	Canada; Mexico
Population:	307,226,000
Largest cities and population:	New York (8,391,881); Los Angeles (3,831,868); Chicago (2,851,268); Houston (2,257,926)
Urban population:	82%
Birth rate:	13.83 per 1,000 people
Life expectancy:	78.1 years (total); 75.7 years (men); 80.7 years (women)
Ethnic groups:	White 79.96% (including 16.3% Hispanic); Black 12.85%; Asian 4.43%; American Indian and Alaska Native 0.97%; Hawaiian 0.18%; Other 1.61%
Religion:	Protestant 51.3%; Roman Catholic 23.9%; None 12.1%; Mormon 1.7%; Jewish 1.7%; Other 9.3%
Internet users:	231,000,000
Military service:	voluntary
Type of government:	**constitution**-based federal **republic**
National animal:	American buffalo
National tree:	oak
Climate:	temperate (mild); tropical in Hawaii and Florida; arctic in Alaska
Total area:	3,794,100 square miles (9,826,675 square kilometers)
Land area:	3,537,455 square miles (9,161,966 square kilometers)
Water area:	256,646 square miles (664,709 square kilometers)
Major mountains:	McKinley; Whitney; St. Helens
Major rivers:	Missouri; Mississippi; Colorado; Ohio
Highest elevation:	Mount McKinley, at 20,322 feet (6,194 meters)
Lowest elevation:	Death Valley, at 282 feet (86 meters) below sea level
Currency:	U.S. dollar ($)

Resources: coal; copper; lead; gold; iron; mercury; oil; natural gas; timber

Major industries: petroleum; steel; vehicles; aerospace; telecommunications; chemicals; electronics; food processing

Imports: clothing; furniture; toys; oil; vehicles

Exports: transistors; aircraft; vehicle parts; fruit; soybeans; corn; computers; medicines

Units of measurements: imperial

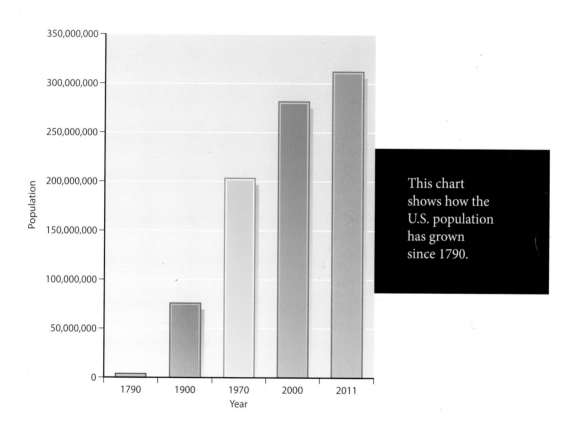

This chart shows how the U.S. population has grown since 1790.

Famous Americans

Mohammed Ali (boxer); Neil Armstrong (astronaut); Hillary Clinton (secretary of state); Tom Cruise (actor); Amelia Earhart (aviation pioneer); Thomas Edison (inventor); Bill Gates (businessman); LeBron James (basketball player); Billie Jean King (tennis player); Martin Luther King (**civil rights** activist); Beyonce Knowles (singer/songwriter); Abraham Lincoln (president); Barack Obama (president); Rosa Parks (civil rights activist); Elvis Presley (singer/songwriter); Franklin D. Roosevelt (president); Pete Sampras (tennis player); Elizabeth Cady Stanton (women's rights activist); Mark Twain (author); George Washington (president); Oprah Winfrey (television personality).

National anthem

The U.S. national anthem is called the "Star Spangled Banner." It was written during the War of 1812, based on words written by Francis Scott Key. **Congress** made the song the official national anthem in 1931.

Oh, say, can you see, by the dawn's early light,

What so proudly we hail'd at the twilight's last gleaming?

Whose broad stripes and bright stars, thro' the perilous fight,

O'er the ramparts we watch'd, were so gallantly streaming?

And the rocket's red glare, the bombs bursting in air

Gave proof thro' the night that our flag was still there.

Oh, say, does that Star-Spangled Banner yet wave

O'er the land of the free and the home of the brave?

National holidays

January 1	New Year's Day
3rd Monday in January	Martin Luther King Day
3rd Monday in February	Presidents' Day
May 30	Memorial Day
July 4	Independence Day
1st Monday in September	Labor Day
2nd Monday in October	Columbus Day
November 11	Veterans' Day
4th Thursday in November	Thanksgiving
December 25	Christmas Day

Fireworks light up the sky over the capital during the annual 4th of July (Independence Day) celebrations.

Timeline

BCE means "before the common era." When this appears after a date, it refers to the number of years before the Christian religion began. BCE dates are always counted backward.

CE means "common era." When this appears after a date, it refers to the time after the Christian religion began.

about 10,000 BCE	The first residents of North America arrive over the Bering Strait.
1492	Christopher Columbus discovers the "new world."
1565	The first permanent European settlement in North America is founded by the Spanish.
1607	Jamestown, Virginia, is founded in present-day Virginia by British settlers.
1773	During the "Boston Tea Party," **colonists** dump British tea into Boston Harbor in protest against British taxes.
1775	George Washington is appointed to lead the fight against British rule. The Revolutionary War begins.
1776	On July 4, Thomas Jefferson's Declaration of Independence is approved by **Congress**; the colonies declare independence.
1783	The Americans defeat the British; the Revolutionary War ends.
1787	The Founding Fathers draw up a new **constitution** for the United States of America; the Constitution comes into effect in 1788.
1789	George Washington is elected the first U.S. president.
1803	The Louisiana Purchase doubles the size of the United States.
1808	The slave trade is **abolished** in the United States.
1846–1848	The United States acquires vast areas of Mexican territory, including present-day California and New Mexico, after the Mexican–American War.
1860–1861	Eleven pro-slavery southern states **secede** from the Union and form the Confederate States of America, triggering the Civil War.
1863	President Abraham Lincoln issues the Emancipation Proclamation, declaring slaves in the Confederate states free.

1865	The Civil War ends; the Confederates are defeated and slavery is abolished. Lincoln is **assassinated**.
1876	Sioux Indians defeat U.S. troops at Little Big Horn.
1890	U.S. troops defeat Sioux Indians at Wounded Knee.
1917	The United States joins the **Allies** to fight in World War I.
1930s	About 13 million people become unemployed after the Wall Street **stock market** crash triggers what becomes known as the Great Depression.
1941	Japanese warplanes attack the U.S. fleet at Pearl Harbor in Hawaii; the United States declares war on Japan and enters World War II.
1945	The United States drops two **atomic** bombs on Hiroshima and Nagasaki; Japan surrenders. World War II ends.
1950–1953	U.S. forces play a leading role against North Korean and Chinese troops in the Korean War.
1954	As a result of the "Brown versus Board of Education of Topeka" Supreme Court case, racial **segregation** in schools is declared unconstitutional. A movement to gain **civil rights** for African Americans begins.
1963	President John F. Kennedy is assassinated.
1968	The civil rights leader Dr. Martin Luther King, Jr., is assassinated.
1969	The United States lands people on the moon for the first time.
1975	After almost 20 years of fighting, the Vietnam War ends.
1991	The United States and allied forces attack Iraq in response to the Iraqi invasion of Kuwait.
2001	**Terrorists** attack the United States and destroy the World Trade Center; over 3,000 people die. The United States invades Afghanistan in response.
2008	Barack Obama is elected the 44th U.S. president.

Glossary

abolition removal or ending

Allies during World Wars I and II, the group of countries that included the United Kingdom, France, and eventually the United States; the Allies fought against Germany

assassinated killed suddenly or secretively, usually for political reasons

atomic relating to the energy of atoms when they are split

capitalist refers to an economic system in which production and distribution are privately owned, and prices are determined by competition in a free market

civil rights right to be treated fairly, regardless of your sex, color, or religion

colonist person who arrives to settle in a new country

communist refers to an economic system in which all means of production and distribution, and all natural resources, belong to the state

Congress branch of the U.S. government that is elected to make laws

constitution set of basic laws by which a country is governed

continent one of Earth's seven major areas of land

developed country country or part of the world with an economy that is more advanced than some other parts of the world

developing country country or part of the world with an economy that is not as advanced as some other parts of the world

diversity having many different kinds or forms

economy relating to money and the industry and jobs in a country

export sell goods to another country

federalism system of government that divides power between the national government and individual state governments

fossil fuel substance such as coal or oil that is burned for fuel

G8 group of industrialized countries, including the United States, Canada, the United Kingdom, and Germany

geyser hot spring that shoots hot water and steam into the air from under the surface

habitat place where plants or animals live

import buy goods from another country

migrate move from one area to another, to find work or settle

multicultural representing many different cultures

Pentagon building that houses the main offices for the armed services of the United States

raw material natural substance that other things are made from

republic country in which there is an elected government and no king or queen

secede withdraw from a group or political union

segregation separating people, usually in racial groups

Senate one half of the U.S. Congress, made up of two senators from each state; the other half of Congress is the House of Representatives

Soviet Union group of countries, including Russia, that made up the Union of Soviet Socialist Republics (USSR)

species type of animal, bird, or fish

stock market market in which shares in businesses are traded

Tagalog language spoken by many people from the Philippines and other areas; it is sometimes referred to as "Filipino"

terrorist person who uses violence to achieve a political aim

tribe group of people who are linked by common ancestry

United Nations global organization formed in 1945 to promote peace and security

urban relating to a town or city

vocational relating to an educational course that provides skills needed for a particular profession

Find Out More

Books

Fiction

Alcott, Louisa M. *Little Women*. New York: Random House, 2005 (first published in 1868 and 1869).

Twain, Mark. *The Adventures of Huckleberry Finn*. New York: Oxford University Press, 2010 (first published in 1884 and 1885).

Nonfiction

Croy, Elden. *United States (Countries of the World)*. Washington, D.C.: National Geographic, 2010.

Fleming, Alice. *Martin Luther King Jr.: A Dream of Hope (Sterling Biographies)*. New York: Sterling, 2008.

Hamilton Murdoch, David. *North American Indian (DK Eyewitness)*. New York: Dorling Kindersley, 2005.

King, David C. *Children's Encyclopedia of American History*. New York: Dorling Kindersley, 2006.

Websites

http://kids.nationalgeographic.com/kids/places/find/united-states-of-america/
Find games, videos, and articles all about the United States here.

http://kids.yahoo.com
Type "United States" into this search engine and find lots of photos, videos, and articles, as well as links to other great sites about the United States.

www.kids.gov
This official U.S. government website provides lots of information about the U.S. government, U.S. history, and more, all written just for kids.

www.usa4kids.com
This website provides interesting information about the United States. You can find out about all of the individual states. There is also a detailed timeline to help you find out about U.S. history.

Places to visit

The Grand Canyon, Arizona
See the amazing natural beauty of the Grand Canyon from above by taking a trip on a helicopter. Afterward you can ride the rapids on the Colorado River at the bottom of the Canyon.

Mount Rushmore, South Dakota
The faces of four presidents—George Washington, Thomas Jefferson, Theodore Roosevelt, and Abraham Lincoln—can be seen carved into the rock face of Mount Rushmore.

California's golden beaches
You can try body boarding or surfing on one of the many golden beaches on the California coast.

Kennedy Space Center, Cape Canaveral, Florida
If you are lucky, you might get to see a rocket setting off on a space mission from the world-famous Kennedy Space Center.

Further research

What did you find interesting in this book? Is there something that you would like to know more about? Here are some topics that you might like to research further:

- Find out about the American Indians and their history, customs, and religions.
- Find out more about slavery in the United States. How did it start, and why? How long did it last? And when was slavery stopped?
- Choose one of the 50 states that you do not know much about and find out more about its people, traditions, food, and places to visit.

You could find out more about the United States by visiting your local library or looking at the websites listed here.

Topic Tools

You can use these topic tools for your school projects. Trace the map onto a sheet of paper, using the thick black outline to guide you. ·

The U.S. flag is called the "Stars and Stripes," and it is easy to see why. Each star represents a state, so there are 50 in all. The 13 stripes represent the 13 original colonies. The flag is sometimes referred to as "Old Glory." Copy the flag design and then color in your picture. Make sure that you use the right colors!

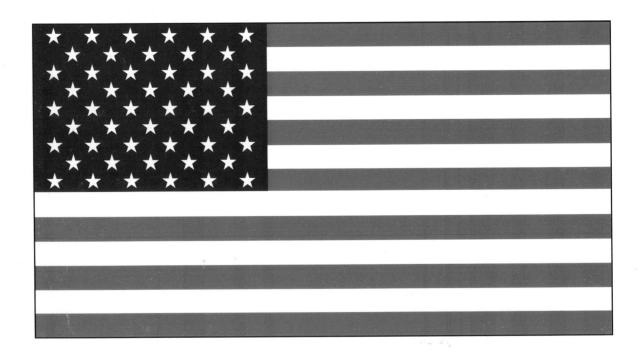

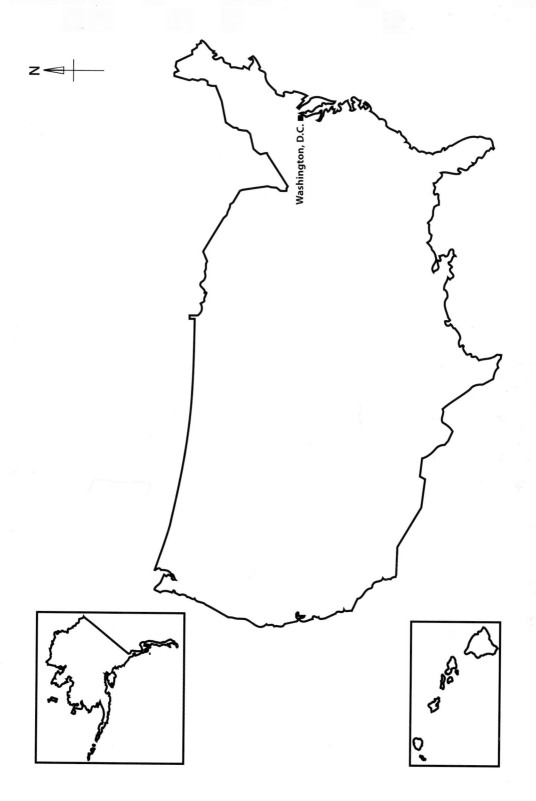

Washington, D.C.

N

Index

agriculture 19
Alaska 14, 15, 16, 20
American Indians 6, 7, 15
area of the United States 4, 36
artists 30

baseball 29
basketball 29
bordering countries 14
Broadway 31

Cabot, John 6
Chicago 16, 36
cities, major 16, 36
civil rights movement 13
Civil War 9
climate 14, 36
Cold War 12
colleges 27
colonies 7
Congress 24
culture 28–33
currency 36

daily life 6, 27
Detroit 18
Disney, Walt 32
Dr. Seuss 33

economy 10, 18–19, 37
education 26–27
environmental issues 22–23
ethnic groups 36
European explorers 6
Everglades 20

famous Americans 38
federalism 24
Fitzgerald, Ella 30, 31
food 28

global influence 4, 34
government 24
Grand Canyon 15, 45
Great Depression 10–11

greenhouse gases 23
greetings 17

health care 24
history 6–13, 40–41
Hollywood 19
Hurricane Katrina 35

immigration 34
imports and exports 34, 37
industries 10, 18–19, 37
infrastructure 24–27
Internet users 36

Jordan, Michael 29

Kansas 19
Kennedy, John F. 12
Kennedy Space Center 45
King, Dr. Martin Luther 13

land uses 18
landscape 15
languages 17
life expectancy 36
literature 33
Los Angeles 16, 36
Louisiana Purchase 8

Mount McKinley 15
mountains 14, 15, 36
movie industry 19, 32
multiculturalism 16, 17, 29, 34
music 30, 31

national anthem 34, 38
national holidays 39
national parks 21
national symbols 36
Native Americans; see
   American Indians
New York 16, 35, 36
North America 4

Obama, Barack 13, 24, 25
oil spills 22

Pearl Harbor 11
Pledge of Allegiance 26
political parties 24
political partners 34
population 4, 36, 37
Puritans 7

recycling 23
religions 36
resources 37
Revolutionary War 8
rivers 14, 36
Roaring Twenties 10

schools 26–27
segregation 13
Senate 24
September 11, 2001, terrorist
   attacks 35
Silicon Valley 19
slavery 9
sports 29
states 16, 17
superpower 4

theater 31
tourism 45
trade agreements 34
Tubman, Harriet 9

Vietnam War 12

wars 8, 9, 10, 11, 12
Washington, D.C. 16
wildlife 20–21, 22
World Wars I and II 10, 11

Yellowstone National Park 21
young people 26–27